THIS IS <u>YOUR</u> DAY!

THIS IS <u>YOUR</u> DAY!

But Everybody Has an Opinion

LISA K. WEISS

with illustrations by

VICTORIA ROBERTS

Villard / New York

Copyright © 1999 by Lisa K. Weiss
Illustrations copyright © 1999 by Victoria Roberts

All rights reserved under International and Pan-American Copyright
Conventions. Published in the United States by Villard Books,
a division of Random House, Inc., New York, and simultaneously
in Canada by Random House of Canada Limited, Toronto.

VILLARD BOOKS and colophon are registered trademarks of Random House, Inc.

Library of Congress Cataloging-in-Publication Data
Weiss, Lisa K.
This is *your* day!: but everybody has an opinion/Lisa K. Weiss with
illustrations by Victoria Roberts.
p. cm.
ISBN 0-375-50265-3 (alk. paper)
1. Weddings—Humor.   2. Weddings—Caricatures and cartoons.
3. American Wit and humor, Pictorial.   I. Roberts, Victoria.   II. Title.
PN6231.W37W45   1999   741.5973—dc21   98-35232

Random House website address: www.atrandom.com
Printed in the United States of America on acid-free paper
2 4 6 8 9 7 5 3
First Edition

Book design by J. K. Lambert

To Joey, my firstborn, whose first solid food was a
    defrosted piece of wedding cake;

To Adam Laughter, my goldenheart, who is the cream
    in my Oreo cookie; and

To Lee Lee, my littlest hon, for being my best girl

L.K.W.

For Mimita

V.R.

Acknowledgments

First, I want to thank my parents for letting it really be *my* day.
I want to thank Victoria Roberts for her brilliance and support.
And I want to thank Michael, for marrying me.

INTRODUCTION

As I sat at the dinner table with my fiancé and his family, conversation quickly turned to wedding plans. His grandmother looked at me gently and bellowed, "I want to wear a forest green satin gown. I've always envisioned the grandmother of the groom in forest green satin. Don't you think that forest green satin will be perfect? The mother of the bride can be in bisque or lavender; the mother of the groom can be in shrimp, but the grandmother of the groom should be in FOREST GREEN SATIN!"

"Yes," I answered tentatively, "that sounds nice, but I haven't decided on the colors of the wedding party yet or even if I'll be in a gown or a short dress. I think that will be okay, but I'll let you know for sure as soon as I figure it out."

"AND," my grandmother-in-law-to-be commanded, "I want to walk down the aisle! The bride's parents always walk down the aisle in a Jewish wedding; the groom's parents walk down the aisle. I WANT TO WALK DOWN THE AISLE!" I nodded and looked helplessly at my intended, unnaturally engrossed in his bean salad.

"AND," bulldozed the grandmother of my beloved, picking up

steam, "I must carry gladiolus. It will look so much better if I carry gladiolus!" "Mmm," I mumbled, in what I hoped would be an appeasing-sounding, inconclusive tone. Better than what? I wondered as I began to squirm.

"AND," my new archenemy pressed forward . . .

Suddenly, a quiet voice dared interrupt. "I suppose you would like to wear a veil, too?"

Silence. Then, explosive laughter from all around the table. At that moment, I thanked God for prospective sisters-in-law.

During the months preceding our wedding, my fiancé and I had to explore countless ideas and negotiate dozens of relationships. We loaded up on wedding planners and advice books, searching for guidance on how to make our wedding tasteful, innovative, and tailored just to us. Through all the well-meant opinions, encouraging advice, and upbeat counsel, a simple refrain rang out over and over and over again: "This is *your* day!"

What a lie.

We found out what every bride and groom learn the hard way: It's not really your day. It's your mother's day. Or your mother-in-law's day. Maybe it's your grandmother-in-law's day. But it isn't simply your day. And the other things they tell you?

They aren't true, either.

THE
WEDDING

This is *your* day!

With all the lovely styles available, you're sure to find a bridesmaid's dress that's becoming to everyone.

Your caterer should be able to
offer you a selection of tantalizing treats
well within your budget.

Now is the time to mend

family feuds.

That dropped waist is so flattering

for every figure type.

With a little organizational skill,

the seating plan can be established easily.

With all that's available, it will be simple to find a flattering headpiece and veil.

Including your pets in the ceremony

can add a warm, cozy touch.

A creative caterer can easily meet

those special dietary requests.

The leg-o'-mutton sleeve

slims any upper arm.

All couples squabble a little bit

before the wedding; it's just nerves.

By the time

your wedding day arrives,

the flower girl

will know just what to do.

If you simply practice beforehand,

your hair will be stunning

on that special day.

Matching bow ties and

cummerbunds are de rigueur.

Just walk naturally

and you'll find you keep time

to the Wedding March.

Asking your best friend

to sing at your wedding is a surefire way

to make the ceremony unique.

It is a delicate and moving tradition

for the bridal couple to feed each other

the first slice of wedding cake.

The bride never eats much

at her own wedding.

THE
HONEYMOON

It's easy to compromise with your beloved

on a final honeymoon destination.

Your boss will be gracious
about giving you time off
for your honeymoon.

Cruises are designed for

honeymooners.

A stay-at-home honeymoon

can give you a jump

on organizing your new home.

Some people enjoy honeymooning

with friends and family.

Those heart-shaped bathtubs

in the Catskill hotels

have never lost their appeal

among the jet set.

A little rain never spoiled

anyone's honeymoon.

Anyone can look sexy

in a silk negligee.

Discovering a heretofore

secret tattoo on your beloved can add

excitement to your honeymoon.

Just because you're on your honeymoon,
there is no reason to forgo your nighttime routine
of exercise, face cream, and hair curlers.

By simply packing your laptop along with your teddies, you can ensure that work anxiety will not intrude upon your honeymoon.

You'll be so involved with each other,

it won't matter where you are.

Exotic food needn't be

a problem on your honeymoon

if you are prepared.

Local characters can add

a romantic touch.

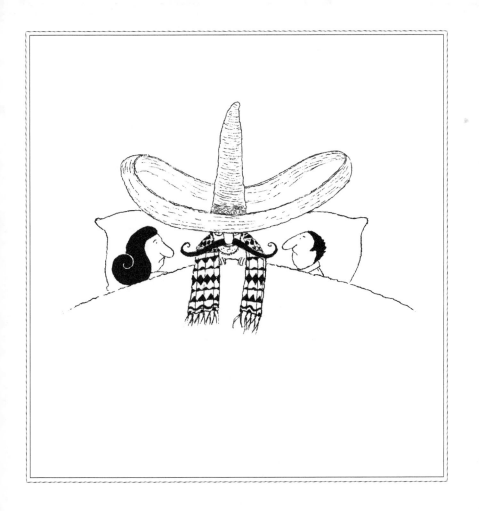

Your spouse will understand

if you need to take along a little work

on your honeymoon.

You'll come back from your honeymoon

relaxed and rested.

THE
NEWLYWEDS

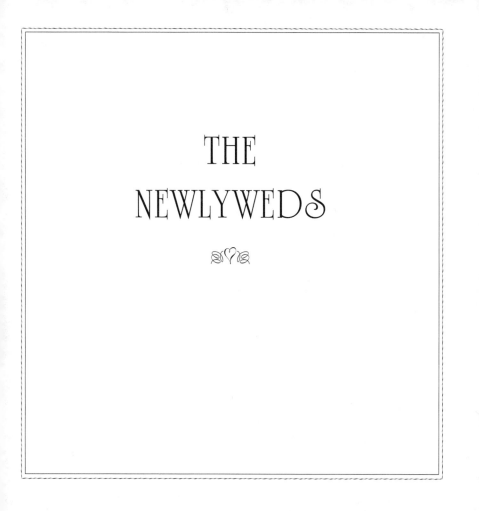

Returning duplicate wedding gifts

can be a pleasant task.

With a little organizational skill,

thank-you notes can be dispatched in no time!

Follow this simple rule

for harmony in the home:

Never go to bed angry.

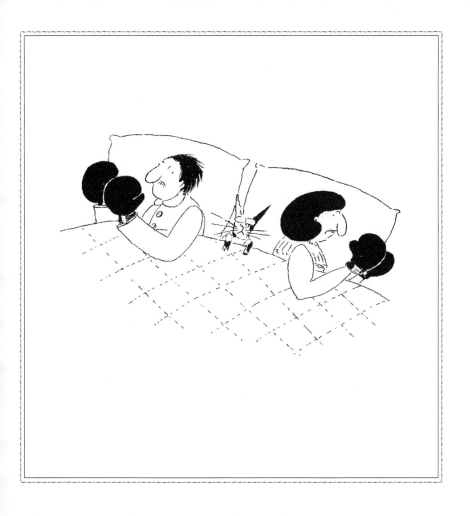

He loves you—he'll get used to how you look in the morning.

Never let her know

what you can do in the kitchen.

These days, figuring out the division

of labor in a marriage is simple.

Living with your parents

can help ease your adjustment

to married life.

Now that you're married, his mother

will be more respectful of you.

Her children will accept you,

as soon as they see how in love you are.

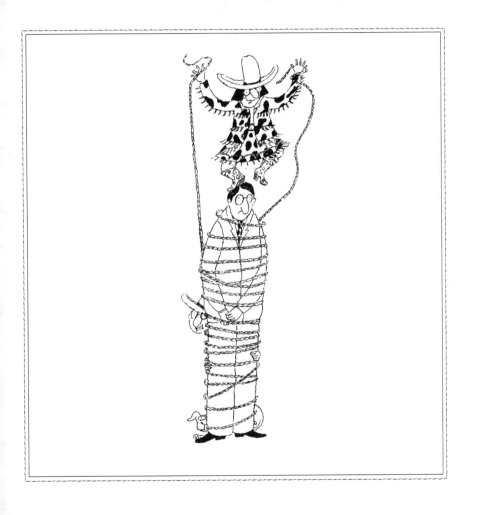

The reappearance of old girlfriends need not

threaten a new marriage.

His ex-wife will lay off

now that you're legally married.

By simply keeping

lines of communication open,

you'll keep conflict at bay.

Now that you're married,

your parents will respect your need for privacy

and won't drop in unless invited.

Cultivating common interests is the key

to a lifetime of togetherness.

Now that you're married,

it will be easy to fine-tune his wardrobe.

Just be spontaneous

and it's easy to keep love alive!